101 Amazing
Do in Austria

C000040814

Introduction

So you're going to Austria, huh? You are very very lucky indeed! You are sure in for a treat because Austria is, without a doubt, one of the most special travel destinations on the face of the planet. It offers something for every visitor, so whether you are into exploring delicious Austrian cheeses, unforgettable adventures in the snow, or celebrating with locals at music festivals, Austria has something for you.

This guide will take you on a journey to all of the major destinations, such as Vienna, Salzburg, Tirol, Carinthia, Innsbruck, Villach, Graz, the Alps, and more besides

In this guide, we'll be giving you the low down on:
- the very best things to shove in your pie hole, whether you want to visit a 1400 seater beer garden in Salzburg or you'd like to go on a cheese tour in the Austrian Alps
- incredible festivals, from the Salzburg Festival, one of the most celebrated arts festivals in Europe, through to an epic dance party in the snow

- the coolest historical and cultural sights that you simply cannot afford to miss like the Baroque gorgeousness of Belvedere Palace through to ancient Roman cities
- the most incredible outdoor adventures, whether you want get your heart racing on a dry toboggan ride, or you want to go scuba diving in a lake
- where to shop for authentic souvenirs so that you can remember your trip to Austria forever
- the places where you can party like a local and make new friends
- and tonnes more coolness besides!

Let's not waste any more time – here are the 101 most amazing, spectacular, and coolest things not to miss in Austria!

1. Pay a Visit to the Clock Museum of Vienna

Vienna is a city that is absolutely packed full of charm, and this is even the case with some of the smaller unique museums that are dotted around the city. One of our favourite places to spend a couple of hours on a rainy afternoon is the Clock Museum. This museum presents one of the most extensive collections of timepieces in all of Europe, with many clocks that date way back to the 1400s. Be sure to be there when the clocks strike on the hour to hear them all chime at once.

(Schulhof 2, 1010 Vienna;
www.wienmuseum.at/de/standorte/uhrenmuseum.html)

2. Fill Yourself Up With Wiener Schnitzel

Wiener Schnitzel might just be the most famous dish in all of Austria, and so, of course, it would be positively criminal to leave the country before chowing down on this simple but incredibly yummy dish. The basic idea is that a cut of veal is butterflied, coated with eggs and breadcrumbs, and fried in lard or clarified butter. Eat it with a simple salad, but never with any kind of sauce – that would be Schnitzel sacrilege in Austria.

3. Take in a Show at the Salzburg Festival

Dating all the way back to 1920, the Salzburg Festival is one of the oldest and most important cultural festivals in all of Austria, and it takes over the city of Salzburg for the end of July and all of August each year. The festival takes over performance venues and outdoor spaces right throughout the year, with everything from classical music to opera to theatre to circus performances. This is one that culture lovers shouldn't miss.

(www.salzburgerfestspiele.at/summer)

4. Surround Yourself With Butterflies in Vienna

Vienna is a city that's well known for its splendour and gorgeous architecture, so it's not a place where you would necessarily expect to have charming experiences in the outdoors. But if you are a nature lover, be sure to find your way to the city's Imperial Butterfly Park, a tropical rainforest and haven for more than 200 species of butterflies. The beautiful creatures will fly all around you and even land on your hands.

(Josefsplatz, 1010 Vienna; www.schmetterlinghaus.at)

5. Take a Dip in a Pool of Beer

Austria is famous for having some really great beers, but the Starkenberger Beer Pools takes beer appreciation to a totally different level. Of course you'll drink lots of beer in Austria, but what about swimming in it? An Austrian brewery has transformed its fermenting beer vats into drinkable pools of beer that you can relax in and drink at the same time. Apparently sitting in beer for an extended period of time is really great for the skin.

(Griesegg 1, 6464 Tarrenz; www.starkenberger.at)

6. Ride the White Water Rapids of the River Inn

Fancy yourself as something of an adventurer? Then there is no question that you need to be familiar with the River Inn, a river that gathers in the Swiss Alps and gains some incredible pace in Austria. This means that it's the perfect spot for thrilling white water rafting. There are Class III and Class V rapids on the river, so there is something for you whether you are a rafting novice or you are experienced on white water.

7. Go Ice Skating on the Frozen Weissensee

Austria is a country with lots and lots of lakes. In the summer, they are beautiful spots for boating or simply gazing out to the water. But in the winter they freeze over, and some of them you can skate on! Weissensee is one of the more popular of these, and it's actually Europe's largest natural ice surface for skating. If you really want to impress, the lake has its own skate school where you can get some fancy skating moves down.

8. Learn About Viennese Murders at Kriminalmuseum

Vienna is such a gorgeous city that you would hardly expect for it to have a dark side, but seek and you shall find, and if you want to explore the dark underbelly of the city, be sure to head to the Kriminalmuseum, which is dedicated to murders in the city. It covers murders from the Middle Ages to the present day, with objects such as bloody gloves, death masks, and rusty axes on display. *(Große Sperlgasse 24, 1020 Vienna; http://wien.kriminalmuseum.at)*

9. Marvel at the Grim Beauty of Eggenburg Charnel

Head out to Eggenburg and you will find something that is equal measures macabre and beautiful: the Eggenburg Charnel. This pit dates back to the end of the 13th century but most of the 5000 bodies were placed there in the 15th century. What makes this charnel so spectacular is just how artfully the bones are arranged to create breath taking symmetrical patterns. It just goes to show that beauty can be created from the darkest of things.

10. Immerse Yourself in a Fake Diamond Fantasia

One of the most famous companies from Austria is Swarovski, producers of crystal and some other related jewellery items. If you're a fan of all things that sparkle, we think you should definitely plan to visit Swaroski Crystal Worlds in Wattens. This fantasia was created in 1995 to celebrate 100 years of the company and consists of 16 different crystal rooms created by different artists who each give their own take on the beauty of Swarovski crystals.

(Kristallweltenstraße 1, 6112 Wattens; https://kristallwelten.swarovski.com)

11. Get Totally Decadent at Restaurant Steirereck

When you're on holiday, it's time to treat yourself, and we think that you deserve at least one fine dining experience in Austria. Restaurant Steirereck in Vienna has been voted as one of the world's top 50 restaurants, so it is most definitely the place to indulge. The restaurant is an ultra-sleek glass cube, and it serves up the most incredible modern Austrian fare. Think freshwater fish from the mountains, and char cooked freshly at your table.

(Am Heumarkt 2A, 1030 Vienna;
www.steirereck.at/en/restaurant)

12. Visit a Medieval Castle Atop a Volcano

There's no shortage of gorgeous historic architecture right around Austria, but Reigersburg Castle really is something out of the ordinary. For a start, this castle is perched right on top of a dormant volcano at a height of 450 metres. The castle dates all the way back to the early 12th century and it's actually made from the asphalt of the volcano itself. Be sure to spend some time there because they have a few fascinating museums dedicated to witchcraft and sorcery.

13. Enter the Largest Ice Cave in the World

If you are something of an adventurer, there's loads of exciting stuff in Austria that goes far beyond cute restaurants and decadent churches. For a day of unbridled adventure, be sure to check out Eisriesenwelt, a natural limestone and ice cave in Werfen that is actually the largest ice cave in the world. Guided tours last for about and a half, and you'll be taken through an underground world of ice formations. Remember to wrap up warm!

(Eishohlenstrasse 30, 5450 Werfen; www.eisriesenwelt.at)

14. Visit an 11th Century Fortress on a Salzburg Hilltop

There are stunning castles to be found right across Austria, and we think that Hohensalzburg Castle in Salzburg is particularly special – in fact, it's the largest fully preserved castle in all of central Europe. The castle is over 900 years old, it's located at a height of more than 500 metres, and it's quite possible to spend the best part of a day exploring all of its nooks and crannies, and enjoying its views of the city, the river, and the surrounding mountains. Take the funicular to the top if you want to save your energy!

(Mönchsberg 34, 5020 Salzburg; www.salzburg-burgen.at/de/hohensalzburg)

15. Try Water-Skiing on Ossiachersee

If the idea of Austria's lakes is appealing to you then it is the Carinthia region where should aim to spend a decent amount of time. You might think that a lake is a lake is a lake, but actually all the lakes in this region have different purposes and attract different types of travellers. If lazing around just makes you bored and you crave adventure, the adventure lake is most definitely Ossiachersee. It's here you can enjoy activities like water skiing, banana tube rides, parasailing, and windsurfing.

16. Get Lost in a Vienna Garden Maze

Schonbrunn Palace is one of the most iconic sites in all of Vienna, but don't just explore the indoor Baroque rooms, because the gardens are also very spectacular. The topiary maze of the Irrgarten is something that's delightful to explore on a sunny day, and kids will love it too. The maze is surprisingly difficult to navigate so don't count on making it out quickly.

(Schönbrunner Schloßstraße 47, 1130 Vienna)

17. Indulge Yourself at the Aqua Dome Langenfeld

When you're on holiday, it's time to indulge and really take care of yourself. And we can't think of anywhere that's more indulgent or relaxing than Aqua Dome Langenfeld, a thermal spa centre that's embedded in the stunning mountain scenery of Otztal. There are two indoor pools with thermal water that comes from the valley, and outdoor spa with thermal pools, a brine pool with underwater music and lighting effects, massage pools, a giant whirlpool, and lots of luxurious treatments as well.

(Oberlängenfeld 140, 6444 Längenfeld; www.aqua-dome.at)

18. Get to Know the Art of Boylesque

Burlesque is something that has become increasingly popular and mainstream over the last twenty years, but have you heard about Boylesque? Well, as the name would suggest, this is like Burlesque dancing but with men instead of women. Believe it or not, this is something that

you can explore in Austria, because each May the
Boylesque Festival is hosted in Vienna, with a mix of great
dancing, acrobatics, striptease, drag, and aerial
performance.

(http://viennaboylesquefestival.com)

19. Check Out Historical Airplanes at Hangar-7

Hangar-7 is definitely one of the more niche places to visit
in Salzburg, but if you have a spare couple of hours and
you have some interest in historical aircraft, we think that
it can be well worth a visit. Inside the stunningly designed
building you'll find 25 historic aircraft, lots of beautiful
Formula One racing cars, and even the original wings with
which sky-jumper Felix Baumgartner crossed the channel.
If you're feeling hungry, there's an innovative gourmet
restaurant on site.

(Wilhelm-Spazier-Straße 7a, 5020 Salzburg; www.hangar-7.com)

20. Be Wowed by Nature at Krimml Falls

There is nobody who doesn't love a good waterfall, and if
you only have time to check out one waterfall in Austria
then you should make sure that it's the Krimml Falls in

the High Tauern National Park. With a height of 380 metres, this is the tallest waterfall in the country, and it's also the most impressive. There is a 4 kilometre waterfall trail in the park with several viewing platforms so you can get the best views and photos of this stunning force of nature.

(www.wasserfaelle-krimml.at)

21. Down a Beer at a Monastery-Run Brewery

There are plenty of monasteries and also plenty of breweries in Austria, and while you wouldn't expect the two to have much in common, you can actually visit a brewery that's managed by a monastery in Salzburg going by the name of Augustiner Braustubl. The monastery was founded for Augustinian hermits in 1605 and has been serving up beer since 1890. It has a delightful garden where you can sip on your beer, and you are even permitted to bring your own food – handy if you're travelling on a budget.

(Lindhofstraße 7, 5020 Salzburg; www.augustinerbier.at)

22. Visit the Former Private Quarters of Sigmund Freud

One of the most famous Austrians in history is, of course, the renowned neurologist and founder of psychoanalysis, Sigmund Freud. While in Vienna, you have the opportunity to learn about the man's life and works at the Sigmund Freud Museum, which is actually located in the former home of the man himself. Inside you'll find many personal items owned by Freud, his antiques, and his patient waiting room. Attached it's the world's largest psychoanalysis library.

(Berggasse 19, 1090 Vienna; www.freud-museum.at/en/)

23. Admire the Medieval Frescoes of Nonnberg Abbey

There are quite a few abbeys strewn across Austria, and frankly, we wouldn't bother to check them all out unless you are really into Monastic culture, but one that we absolutely love is Nonnberg Abbey. This Benedictine Abbey in Salzburg is the oldest women's abbey in Europe, and it has been in constant use since it was founded in 714. There are some stunning religious frescoes inside, and some of the scenes from the Sound of Music were shot there.

(Nonnberggasse 2, 5020 Salzburg; www.benediktinerinnen.de)

24. Explore the Underground Cave System of Seegrotte

Austria is a stunning country with many natural attractions, and you can even find an immense amount of beauty underneath the earth itself. Seegrotte is an underground cave system in the small town of Hinterbruhl, and there's even a series of underground canals that make up Europe's largest subterranean lake. It is possible to take boat trips on the lake and explore this underground wonder.

(Grutschgasse 2a, 2371 Hinterbrühl; www.seegrotte.at)

25. Explore a Collection of Useless Inventions

With all the grand palaces and stately churches, Austria can seem like a pretty serious place, but one place you can visit for a little bit of light relief is Nonseum, a museum that is completely dedicated to useless inventions. This museum is tucked away in the small town of

Herrnbaumgarten, but we think that it's well worth a morning of your time. Inside you can find rounded scissors for "faster haircuts" and a hat that opens at the top. You're guaranteed to leave with a smile on your face. *(Poysbrunner Str. 9, 2171 Herrnbaumgarten; www.nonseum.at)*

26. Pay a Visit to the World's Oldest Salt Mine

When you imagine your vacation, you probably don't imagine descending into the depths of a salt mine, but if you want to comprehend local history we think that a trip into the Hallein Salt Mine is well worth the effort. This salt mine has been worked for around 7000 years, since the times of the Celtic tribes. A 90 minute guided tour will teach you about the history, and even take you on a boat trip on a lake inside the mine.

(Ramsaustraße 3, 5422 Bad Dürrnber; www.salzwelten.at)

27. Eat a Typical Austrian Sausage, Kasekrainer

When in Central Europe, eat plenty of sausage, right? Right. But there are so many different types of sausages that eating them all on one holiday might just cause you to explode. Probably worth it, but still if you only have the chance to sample one kind of sausage that is local to Austria make sure that it's Kasekrainer. This is a pure pork sausage with a little bit of bacon, and lots of garlic and black pepper. It is hot smoked, heat cured, and eaten with mustards.

28. Be Wowed by a Stunning Baroque Church in Vienna

If church architecture is what you are into, you are going to have a ball during your time in Austria. While Karlskirche is not even close to being the oldest church in Vienna, it is one of the most beautiful, and it also has a fascinating story. This church was constructed in the early 18th century as a way to give thanks for the passing of the plague epidemic. It's also an architectural curiosity with a mix of ancient Greek and Roman aspects, combined with Byzantine, Baroque, and Renaissance stylings.

(Kreuzherrengasse 1, 1040 Vienna)

29. Eat at the Oldest Restaurant in Central Europe

Located within the walls of St Peter's Abbey, the Stfitskeller St Peter restaurant really is one of a kind. In fact, it can actually claim to be the oldest restaurant in all of central Europe. And actually, some claims suggest that it's the oldest restaurant in the world. For that reason alone, it's well worth checking out. We recommend the weekly Mozart dinners with live music and staff wearing period costumes.

(Sankt-Peter-Bezirk 1, 5020 Salzburg; www.stpeter.at/en/the-restaurant.html)

30. Spend the Night in a Sewer Pipe

Spending the night in a sewer sounds like the exact opposite of a good time, but wait and hear us out for a moment because the Dasparkhotel is a one-of-a-kind accommodation experience that you won't want to miss. Industrial drainage pipes are huge and very durable. This means that when they are discarded they don't biodegrade. And so some clever people in Austria thought to upcycle these pipes and create unique hotel rooms from them. Ys, they were once sewer pipes, but now they are surprisingly comfortable.

(Rodlstraße 21, 4100 Ottensheim; www.dasparkhotel.net)

31. Check out Local Modern Art at Kunsthaus Graz

As you traverse the art scene of Austria, you would probably expect to mostly see the Old Masters and classic paintings, but actually there is a whole world of contemporary art to be explored as well, and one of the best spots to see a more cutting edge arts scene is at the Kunsthaus Graz. There are many rotating exhibitions, but even more impressive is the building itself, which sort of looks like a glistening robot heart from the future. It's embedded with 1000 fluorescent discs that provide captivating light shows after dark.

(Lendkai 1, 8020 Graz; www.museum-joanneum.at/en/kunsthaus-graz)

32. Warm Yourself With a Piping Hot Bowl of Rindsuppe

For us, Rindsuppe is the perfect autumnal food, and if you want to warm yourself from the inside out without weighing yourself down with something really heavy, Rindsuppe is the perfect dish without a doubt. This is a simple clear beef broth and what it lacks in complex ingredients it makes up for in sheer deliciousness. Cooked with beef bones and a few root vegetables, it's packed full of flavour.

33. Enjoy the Tremendous Skiing Runs of Alpbach

If winter sports give you life, you already know that Austria is an awesome destination for things like skiing, snowboarding, and skating, but actually there's so much choice for winter resorts that it can be a little tricky to know which one to choose. For us, Alpbach is always a reliable choice. It's located in a small village in Tyrol, so it's a "get away from it all" kind of place, but it still has lots of adventure with great ski runs, and also some lovely hiking paths if you want to take things easy and just enjoy the mountain landscapes.

(www.alpbachtal.at/en)

34. Fill Your Stomach With Yummy Knodel Dumplings

Different types pf dumplings can be found all over the world, but Central Europe is a part of the world where they are very popular, and a particular type of dumpling that you'll find all over Austria is the Knodel. These bread dumplings are very simple and just made with bread, milk, eggs, salt, and chives, and that can be included in or eaten with a variety of dishes such as mushroom ragout or a hearty goulash.

35. Step Back in Time at Otzi-Dorf

If you are the kind of person who just finds it hard to get on board with stuffy museums because all the exciting stuff is kept inside glass cages, then you might have more luck with Otzi-Dorf, which is like a museum that is brought completely to life. This is an outdoor archaeological park that is dedicated to the Iceman, a glacial mummy discovered in the Alps. You'll find traditional thatched dwellings, recreations of late-Neolithic graves, craft displays, and even areas where wild boar and oxen roam freely.

(Am Tauferberg 8, 6441 Umhausen; www.oetzi-dorf.at)

36. Ascend the World's Tallest Wooden Observation Deck

There is no doubt that Austria has some of the most breath-taking landscapes that you can find anywhere in

Europe, but you can't fully appreciate the beauty of Austria when you have a worm's eye view on the ground, and so we heartily recommend ascending to the heights of the Pyramidenkogel Tower, which is the world' tallest wooden observation deck. Ascend the 2700 feet above sea level and you'll have the most spectacular view of the mountains all around and even into neighbouring Slovenia.

(Linden 62, 9074 Linden; www.pyramidenkogel.info)

37. Explore a World of Miniatures at Minimundus

Head to Minimindus, and you'll feel as though you have travelled all over the world in just one afternoon. This park specialises in miniatures of some of the most iconic buildings all around the world at a ratio of 1:25. These miniatures are crafted by expert model makers, and their detail really is something to behold. In the park, you can find miniatures of the Eiffel Tower, St Petersburg Cathedral, the White House and more.

(Villacher Str. 241, 9020 Klagenfurt am Wörthersee; www.minimundus.at/en)

38. Eat Austrian Comfort Food, Spatzle & Nockerl

Austria can be really quite cold for a good portion of the year, especially if you are up high in the mountains, and so this is a country that really knows how to do comfort food, and it doesn't get much more comforting than a heaped bowl of Spatzle & Nockerl. The basic idea is that these are hearty egg noodles served with cheese, so you can think of it as the Austrian version of Mac n Cheese. If you're feeling adventurous, it's also often eaten with sauerkraut.

39. Explore the Baroque Interiors of Schonbrunn Palace

No trip to Vienna would be complete without exploring one of its most iconic attractions, Schonbrunn Palace. This former summer imperial palace is one of the most important architectural, historical, and cultural monuments in the country, and with an astounding 1441 Baroque rooms, it will take some time to explore! There is so much to cover that we would absolutely recommend taking one of the excellent guided tours so that you can see the highlights and get to know the important history of the palace.

(Schönbrunner Schloßstraße 47, 1130 Vienna;
www.schoenbrunn.at/en)

40. Pick Up Ceramics at the Potters' Market in Hall

Austria is known for some beautiful buildings and gorgeous scenery, but what about the local culture of handicrafts? If you are the artsy type, then you may want to schedule your trip for the end of August when a Potters' Market is held in a town called Hall in the Tyrol region. The market attracts ceramics artists from all over Austria and beyond, and it's the perfect place to indulge and purchase something to treasure forever.

(www.tyrol.tl/en/calendar/details/hall-pottery-market)

41. Ride the Wiener Riesenrad Ferris Wheel

In our opinion, one of the most charming ways of getting to know the landscape of Vienna is by taking a ride on the Riesenrad Ferris Wheel. This Big Wheel dates all the way back to the late 19th century and is still spinning today – in fact, it was the tallest Ferris Wheel in the world from 1920 to 1985. If you're feeling particularly fancy, there are VIP gondolas that can be booked where you will be served a luxurious dinner.

(Riesenradplatz 1, 1020 Vienna; www.wienerriesenrad.com)

42. Go Scuba Diving in the Green Lake

Austria is a country that is totally different at different times of the year. Visit the Green Lake in the winter, and you'll see an iced over vision. In the summer, not only does the ice melt, but the snowmelt from surrounding mountains floods the lake, and its depth increases from 1 metre to 12 metres. This makes it a unique but special diving destination in the summer months, and you can even take underwater photography courses there.

43. Party in the Snow at Snowbombing Festival

Book your tickets for the Snowbombing Festival and you will soon realise that Austria is a country that truly has it all – snow, sunshine, and the ability to party hard like no other. Snowbombing is hosted each year at the Mayrhofen Ski Resort in November at the beginning of April, set against the most stunning backdrop of snowy mountain peaks. You can rave in igloos, party in enchanted forests, and dance to music from the likes of Chase & Status, Mark Ronson, and Tinie Tempah.

(http://snowbombing.com)

44. Take in all the Decadence of Belvedere in Vienna

The Belvedere is a historic building complex with no less than two Baroque palaces, and it's the very epitome of Viennese elegance and refinement. As well as an incredible building, The Belvedere plays host to the most comprehensive collection of Austrian art to be found anywhere, with pieces from the Middle Ages to the present day. On a summer's day, the manicured gardens are very pleasant for a stroll too.

(Schloss Belvedere, Prinz Eugen-Straße 27, 1030 Vienna; www.belvedere.at/en)

45. Ride the Alpine Coaster Golm

Do you have the need for speed? Then we are in no doubt that you will have the time of your life riding the Alpine Coaster Golm, which is a winter and summer toboggan run that's safe for the whole family to enjoy. You will reach speeds of up to 40 kilometres/hour, there's no less

than 15 hair-raising hairpin turns, and 44 exciting jumps
that will land your heart in your mouth.

(Latschaustraße 62, 6774 Tschagguns;
www.golm.at/en/active/Alpine-Coaster-Golm)

46. Say Hi to the Animals at Vienna Zoo

A day at the zoo is always a treat, but Vienna Zoo,
otherwise known as the Tiergarten Schonbrunn is a
particularly special treat because this is the oldest zoo in
the entire world, dating back to the mid 18th century.
There's more than 750 animals here with many exotic
species such as giant pandas, Siberian tigers, emus, and
more. There are feedings throughout the day, which are
always fascinating to watch.

(Maxingstraße 13b, 1130 Vienna; www.zoovienna.at/en/zoo-and-
visitors/visitor-information)

47. Get Decadent With a Plate of Kaischerschmarrn

When you're on holiday, it's time to get decadent and treat
yourself to the fatty carb-filled foods that you wouldn't
normally allow yourself to eat at home. And for a stomach
pleasing treat like no other, we love to indulge in

Kaischerschmarrn. These are fluffy pancakes that are baked in butter, shredded, and then served with apple sauce. Forget about calories for a day, eh?

48. Get to Grips With Modern Austrian Art at the Leopold Museum

The Leopold Museum holds one of the largest collections of contemporary Austrian art in the whole country, and while it's not one of the best known museums in Vienna, it's definitely worth visiting if you are especially interested in the local art scene. Some of the Austrian artists on display include Gustav Klimt, Egon Schiele, Oskar Kokoschka, and Richard Gerstl. There are guided tours in English every Sunday afternoon.

(Museumsplatz 1, 1070 Vienna; www.leopoldmuseum.org/en)

49. Escape City Life in the Gorgeous Volksgarten

While Vienna is not exactly a city with a lot of hustle and bustle, if you are a nature lover there are still some places that you can escape to, and we particularly love the Volksgarten, which is the garden attached to the Hofburg Palace. The gardens were created between 1817 and 1821, and have been open to the public since way back in 1823. The park is famous for its rose garden, which plays host to more than 3000 rose bushes, and there is even a coffee house in the park where you can have your morning caffeine fix.

(http://volksgarten.at/en)

50. Take in a Classical Concert at Wiener Musikverein

Classical music is a big deal in Austria. This country is, after all, the birthplace of famous composers like Mozart. And so this is truly a haven for classical music buffs with plenty of outstanding venues where you can enjoy live performances. One of the most renowned of these venues in Vienna is the Wiener Musikverein, which dates back to 1870, and is the official home of the Vienna Philharmonic Orchestra. With regard to its incredible acoustics, this is regarded as one of the best concert halls in the world.

(Musikvereinsplatz 1, 1010 Vienna; www.musikverein.at)

51. Get to Know Vienna's Market Culture at Naschmarkt

One of our favourite ways of getting to know its city is by immersing itself in its market culture, and when in Vienna, it's Naschmarkt that you simply have to visit. This market is vast, and it sells pretty much everything. There are sections dedicated to antiques and vintage items, stalls selling fresh food of all kinds, street food stalls, and there's even live DJ entertainment. It opens Monday to Saturday, but is bigger on Saturdays.

(www.wien.gv.at/freizeit/einkaufen/maerkte/lebensmittel/naschma rkt)

52. Explore a World of Exotic Plants at Palmenhaus Schonbrunn

With chilly winters and fresh summers, Austria is one of the last places where you would expect to find exotic plants and flowers, but this is a country that has it all, and you could be mistaken for thinking you are in the tropical green of Costa Rica at the Palmenhaus Schonbrunn, a huge greenhouse in Vienna. It contains more than 4500 plant species, so there is plenty to explore, and notable plants include a coco de mer, which only blossoms every 50-100 years, and a 350 year old olive tree.

*(Schlosspark Schönbrunn, 1130 Vienna;
www.schoenbrunn.at/wissenswertes/der-schlosspark/rundgang-
durch-den-park/palmenhaus.html)*

53. Go Canoeing on the River Danube

The River Danube, the second longest river in Europe, runs through many countries including Austria Hungary, Slovakia, and Croatia, and is one of the most iconic rivers in the world. There are many ways to enjoy this beautiful expanse of water, but the best way to completely immerse yourself in the river landscape is by taking a canoe trip out on the water. We think the best place for a canoe ride on the river is in the Donau National Park, because it's a lot less trafficked than the river in Vienna.

54. Dance the Waltz at the Vienna Opera Ball

There is nowhere that stages a grand ball quite in the way that the city of Vienna does. These balls are grand, lavish affairs that attract local high society, and people who are attracted to the more decadent things in life from all over the world. The Vienna Opera Ball is the ball of all balls. Be sure to purchase tickets in advance, dress up in your finest clothes, and learn the waltz before you show up! The ball takes place each year at the beginning of February. *(www.wiener-staatsoper.at/en/vienna-opera-ball)*

55. Eat the Best Apple Strudel of Your Life at Café Hawelka

Austria is better known for savoury than sweet dishes, but there is one Austrian dessert that has made waves all over the world, and that's the apple strudel. Be sure to eat it wherever you can find it across the country, but we'd traverse the Alps to have a slice of the good stuff at Café Hawelka in Vienna. The traditional Viennese café opened all the way back in 1939 and used to be a meeting point for famous writers like Konrad Bayer and Ernst Fuchs. It's still run by the same family.

(Dorotheergasse 6, 1010 Vienna; www.hawelka.at/cafe)

56. Take in the View from the Dachstein Sky Walk

When you travel to a different country, this is the time to experience things that you would never normally experience at home – so how about walking along an elevated skywalk in the crevice of a glacier? That's exactly what you can do with the Dachstein Sky Walk. Walk along to the edge, and you'll be presented with a 250 metre sheer rock face beneath you. This isn't one for people with vertigo, but if you can handle the butterflies in your stomach, it will be worth braving.

(www.derdachstein.at/en/dachstein-glacier-world/glacier-experience/skywalk)

57. Party All Night at Electric Love Festival

If your favourite thing in the world is to dance to the sounds of banging electronic music all night long, then you should book your tickets to the annual Electric Love Festival as a matter of priority. It takes place every July at a race course in Salzburg, and it's a festival that truly unites electronic music lovers from right across Europe, whether you're into Dubstep, Hardstyle or Italo Disco. Previous acts that have graced the stage include David Guetta, Hardwell, and Dimitri Vegas.

(www.electriclove.at/en)

58. Go Birdwatching at Lake Neusiedl

The lakes of Austria are not just places where you can relax and go on boat trips, they are also home to lots of local wildlife including an immense number of birds. If you are a keen birdwatcher, the lake that you simply can't miss is Lake Neusiedl in the east part of the country. In fact, you can even go on a birdwatching safari here to check out over 300 different species of birds, from eagles to tiny chiffchaffs.

59. Take an Eerie Trip Into the Stephansdom Crypt

There's no shortage of gorgeous churches in Vienna, and St Stephen's, or Stephansdom, might just be the most beautiful of them all. But look beyond the façade and you can explore something that's altogether more creepy. Beneath the stone floors lie the remains of 11,000 people, and in fact, the crypt is still an active burial spot. The really creepy thing about the crypt is that you can find the hearts and intestines of princes, emperors, and queens kept in jars.

(Stephansplatz 3, 1010 Vienna; www.stephanskirche.at)

60. Explore All the Grandeur of Mirabell Palace

If you have limited time in Salzburg and you want to explore the most iconic sights, be sure to include the Mirabell Palace in your list of must-visits, because it truly is worth making a priority. It was first built in 1606 but extended and revamped in glorious Baroque style in the 18th century to become the Palace as it is known today. You can enter for free and explore the gorgeous stucco, marble, and frescoes all around. But the gardens also deserve a lot of your time, and you might even recognise part of the gardens from scenes in the Sound of Music. *(Mirabellplatz, 5020 Salzburg)*

61. Be Wowed by a Royal Collection of Art and Treasure

Arts lovers will be in Seventh Heaven on a trip to Austria, and the Kunsthistoriches Museum bears endless exploration. If you have a limited amount of time, we'd recommend heading straight to the Kunstkammer Wien room, which is dedicated to showcasing the curiosities and art objects amassed by the Habsburgs. The collection represents pure luxury and opulence with objects such as carved rhinoceros horns, tapestries, scientific instruments, and carved ivory sculptures.

(Maria-Theresien-Platz, 1010 Vienna; www.khm.at/en/visit/collections/kunstkammer-wien)

62. Wave a Rainbow Flag at Vienna Pride

If you're an LGBT traveller visiting Austria, you might wonder what a trip to Austria can offer you. You'll be pleased to know that the country is largely tolerant and you can find gay bars all over the country, but if you really want to celebrate we recommend heading to the capital city for Vienna Pride in June. There are lots of fun events during Pride week but it all peaks with an incredible parade through the streets full of glitter, colour, dancing, music, and an abundance of unabashed pride.
(www.viennapride.at)

63. Get Close to Monkeys at Affenberg Landskron

Austria is probably one of the last places on the planet that you would expect to find monkeys, but seek and you shall find, and if you are a wildlife lover then head to Affenberg Landskron just outside of the city of Villach. The really great thing about this place is that there are no cages or circus tricks, just beautiful Barbary macaques that are free to roam, and you can enjoy a guided tour to get to know more about their lives in the Austrian forest.

(Schloßbergweg 18, 9523 Gratschach; www.affenberg.com)

64. Scale the Heights of Hochosterwitz Castle

Look, we know that there are so many castles in Austria that there is potential to get castle-d out pretty easily, but if you just can't get enough and really want to get into the local history, we'd recommend Hochosterwitz Castle, which is one of the more impressive medieval castles, basically in the middle of nowhere. It dates bate to 860, and very few changes have been made to it since the 17th century. It's 664 metres above sea level and offers a spectacular view.

(Hochosterwitz 1, 9314 Launsdorf; www.burg-hochosterwitz.com)

65. Drive Austria's High Alpine Road

If you want to get outside of the main cities, it can be really useful to hire a rental car, and there are some really spectacular drives that you can take so that your time in the car becomes an event to remember in itself. The High Alpine Road is one of the best known drives in the country, and with good reason. The road ascends through the mountains and takes a number of hairpin curves, but it's worth it if you're confident behind the wheel.

66. Tour the Austrian Parliament Building

Whether you have an interest in politics, history, beautiful buildings, or all three of those things, the Austrian Parliament Building in Vienna is a definite must-visit. The building was completed in 1884, and was constructed in the traditional Greek style to represent the Hellenic ideals of law and freedom. To view the interior of the building you'll have to book a guided tour, which is well worth doing if you really want to get under the skin of the city. *(Dr.-Karl-Renner-Ring 3, 1017 Vienna; www.parlament.gv.at)*

67. Catch a Show at the Bregenz Festival

Bregenz is a small Austrian city on the edge of Lake Constance that is not particularly well known on the tourist scene, but it comes to life in July and August when the Bregenz Festival, an annual performing arts festival, takes place. There are performances in all kinds of locations, but are particularly special at Seebuhne, a floating amphitheatre that can host 7000 spectators, normally for grand opera performances. There's over 100 shows each year so you're bound to find something you want to see.

(https://bregenzerfestspiele.com/en)

68. Explore a Baroque Library of the Hapsburg Empire

Any bibliophile that finds themselves in Austria simply has to visit the Austrian National Library in the Hofburg Palace in Vienna. This is the largest library in Austria, but size isn't everything, and what really makes this place a must-visit is its astounding Baroque beauty. The library dates all the way back to the early 18th century, and has accumulated a collection of more than 7 million books since then.

(Josefsplatz 1, 1015 Vienna; www.onb.ac.at)

69. Spend Way Too Much Money at the Ursulamarkt

One of the best ways to get to know a local culture, and too indulge an inner shopaholic is by getting to know the local markets of the places you visit. In Austria, we can highly recommend Ursulamarkt, a market which is always held in October in the Carinthia region. This market dates back an astonishing 700 years, and it's the ideal spot for souvenir shopping because you can find local crafts like ceramics and wooden toys.

70. Get Inspired by Vienna's Windows for Peace

Vienna's Peace Museum is undoubtedly one of the most inspiring places in the whole capital, hosting regular discussions, debates, and exhibits related to peace. But their most significant exhibition is permanent and open for everyone to see on the streets of Vienna because the Windows for Peace are located on the exterior of the building. Each of the windows represents an iconic "Peace Hero" such as Gandhi, Nelson Mandela, and Malala Yousafzai.

(Blutgasse 3, 1010 Vienna;
www.peacemuseumvienna.com/windows-for-peace)

71. Hike Through the Wilder Kaiser Mountain Range

If you love nothing more than to strap on your hiking boots and feel your lungs fill up with fresh mountain air,

Austria is a must visit destination. To be honest, pick a mountain and you can walk it, but we particularly love the Wilder Kaiser Mountain Range for its 400 kilometres of well marked hiking paths. You can enjoy day hikes, or if you want something more intensive, there are huts dotted around the trails so you can walk from hut to hut over a series of days.

72. Sample Deliciousness on the Bregenzerwald Cheese Trail

Who doesn't love to chow down on a hulk of cheese? Crazy people. That's why you need to know about Bregenzerwald Cheese Trail, which combines two of our favourite things in life – glorious cheese and stunning local scenery. This trail gathers together farms, cheesemakers, restaurants and eateries, and alpine dairymen so cheese lovers like you can have the ultimate cheese experience. You'll get to learn about traditional cheesemaking practices, you can eat lots of the good stuff, and learn some interesting cheese recipes while enjoying all the beauty of Alpine Austria.

(www.bregenzerwald.at/s/en/kaesestrasse-bregenzerwald)

73. Enjoy Winter Activities at the Stubai Glacier

One of the really cool things about Austria is how different it is from season to season, and if you'd rather wrap up warm in the mountains than swelter on a beach, the Stubai Glacier is a must-visit destination in the winter months. This is actually the largest glacier ski resort in the whole country, and there's a whole lot to keep you entertained. It's also one of the most kid-friendly resorts in Austria with special instructors for kids and even a kids' snow obstacle course.

74. Take a Dip in Millstatter See

In our opinion, one of the loveliest things about Austria is its abundance of natural lakes, which are the perfect places for relaxed and serene getaways. There's so many great lakes that it's hard to pick, but we think that Millstatter See is extra special. There's all kinds of things to enjoy there, from biking around the edge of the lake to dining on the floating restaurant. But we especially love diving into its waters, which are known to be some of the warmest in the country.

75. Put Your Foot to the Pedal on the Danube Cycle Path

The Danube is one of the most iconic rivers in Europe, running through much of the central part of the continent, and what better to way to take all of its gloriousness in while getting some great exercise than by putting your foot to the pedal and cycling along the edge of the river? Fortunately, there is a dedicated cycle path that can take you from the north to the south of the country, and beyond if you want an even grander adventure.

76. Rock Til You Drop at Nova Rock Festival

These days, summer music festivals tend to be geared towards fans of electronic music, but if you're a rocker at heart you don't have to miss out on the festival fun, because Austria has an awesome annual rock festival called Nova Rock. It's located in Burgenland close to the Hungarian border, and attracts rockers from right across Europe. Bands that have performed at Nova Rock in the past include The Prodigy, Iron Maiden, and Black Sabbath, to name just a few legendary artists.

(www.novarock.at)

77. Down Some Beer at Austria's Largest Beer Inn

A trip to Austria without a few glasses of beer is really not a trip to Austria at all, and if you only have the opportunity to make it to one of Austria's famous beer inns, it stands to reason that you would choose the largest beer inn in the country – Augustiner Brau. With 1400 seats in its garden, you'll have no problem finding somewhere to sit even on the sunniest of Salzburg afternoons. There's often live music too, and we can't think of anywhere we'd rather sip a pint in Austria.

(Lindhofstraße 7, 5020 Salzburg; www.augustinerbier.at/?L=1)

78. Explore Some Incredible Dance at ImPulsTanz Festival

For five weeks of the year, Vienna turns into the dance capital of the world when the ImPulsTanz Festival takes of the city. The festival typically runs from mid July to mid August and it attracts thousands of dance professionals, teachers, and students. As well as having the chance to see some cutting edge dance performances, there's a whole bunch of dance workshops that cater to dance beginners and pros alike.

(www.impulstanz.com/en)

79. Get All Dressed Up for a Night at the Vienna State Opera

If you love a reason to put on your very best clothes and enjoy a night on the town, there are plenty of gorgeous places to show off a beautiful cocktail dress or sharp tuxedo in Vienna, and where could possibly be better than the Vienna State Opera? Whether you would like to see an opera, a ballet performance, or a classical concert, the choice is yours. And everybody gets dressed up here, so you won't feel out of place in your Sunday best.

(Opernring 2, 1010 Vienna; www.wiener-staatsoper.at)

80. Get Back to Nature at Feldkirch Wildpark

Austria is that country that just has it all. So when you have had your fill of opulent palaces and dramatic church architecture you can head out into the country and feel the wonder of the outdoors in places like Feldkirch Wildpark. Whether you want to take a run in some fresh air, you want a leisurely stroll in nature, or you want to get close to animals such as marmots, ibex, and wild boar, this is the spot.

(Feldkirch Wildpark; www.wildpark-feldkirch.at)

81. Chow Down on Tafelspitz at Plachutta in Vienna

Because Vienna is a capital city, it's a place where you can find many different types of cuisines, but make sure you visit at least one traditional restaurant, and Plachutta is a family run restaurant that is well known for serving up lots of traditional Viennese yumminess. This restaurant specialises in a dish called Tafelspitz, which is either boiled veal or beef in broth served with minced apples and horseradish.

(Wollzeile 38, 1010 Vienna; www.plachutta-wollzeile.at)

82. Raise Your Adrenaline on the Airrofan Sky Glider

Want to get your heart pumping and have some serious adventure while you're in Austria? Activities like skiing and snowboarding are great, but you can take the adrenaline rush to the next level by taking a flight on the Airrofan Sky Glider. When you are harnessed into this unique contraption, you get to glide over the Alps horizontally and you will reach speeds of up to 80 kilometres/hour. Do you dare?

(www.rofanseilbahn.at)

83. Delve Into a World of Art Forgery in Vienna

In an iconic capital city like Vienna you would expect there to be plenty of art museums, and indeed there are, but the most unusual of all these would have to be the Museum of Art Fakes. Of course, there is great skill in being able to create a copy of a renowned piece of art and pull the wool over many people's eyes, and this museum is dedicated to those accomplished forgeries. This is a place that will make you question the very idea of art, its value, what is real, and what isn't.

(Löwengasse 28, 1030 Vienna; www.faelschermuseum.com)

84. Indulge a Sweet Tooth With Palatschinken

When you think of Austrian food, you no doubt think of sausages, smoked cheeses, and Schnitzel? But what if you have more of a sweet tooth? Have no fear because Austria is not going to let you down. Seek out a plate of glorious

Palatschinken and all will be well with the world. These are essentially the Central European version of a crepe, and they are typically filled with plum or apricot jam and dusted with powdered sugar.

85. Take in a View of Vienna From Donauturm

Vienna, in our opinion, is one of the most breath takingly beautiful cities anywhere in Europe, and the best way of taking in all of that beauty is at a great height. That's why we would whole heartedly recommend ascending the Donauturm, which is the tallest structure in the city with a height of 252 metres. There is a viewing platform at a height of 150 metres, which a high speed elevator will take you to in just 35 seconds, but you can climb to the top if you are feeling particularly fit and healthy. The observation deck also offers bungee jumping if you're the adventurous sort.

(Donauturmstraße 8, 1220 Vienna; www.donauturm.at/en)

86. Have a Fun Day at the World's Oldest Amusement Park

Travelling with kids is a double edged sword. You need to go to special efforts to keep them entertained, which can be exhausting, but it's so rewarding to create those memories for them. Somewhere you can take them for the day and know they'll have a great time is Wurstelprater in Vienna. Unbeknownst to them you'll also be giving them a history lesson because this is the oldest amusement park in the whole world, dating all the way back to 1776.

(www.praterwien.com/en/home)

87. Go Underground an Explore the Obir Dripstone Caves

If you want a true adventure while you're in Austria be sure to head underground and explore the Obir Dripstone Caves, a magical natural sight in Austria that not too many tourists (or locals for that matter) seem to know about. These caves were discovered back in 1870 by miners who were digging for lead, and you can still see their tracks today. The hanging stalactites are stunning, and perfectly illuminated beneath the ground.

(www.hoehlen.at/en)

88. Hit a Few Golf Balls at Golfclub Am Mondsee

For some people, a great holiday means venturing from museum to museum, for some it means eating as much of the local food as is humanly possible, and for others the simple pleasure of spending time on the golf course is the greatest pleasure of all. If you fall into the latter category, there's no shortage of wonderful golf courses across the Austrian landscape, and we particularly love Golfclub Am Mondsee. Its 18 holes are situated right on the edge of a lake, and there are mountain views to enjoy while you get that hole-in-one.

(St. Lorenz 400, 5310 St. Lorenz; www.mondsee.golf)

89. Visit a Bizarre Looking Cubist Church

Church architecture is something that you can find plenty of in Austria, with churches dating way back to Medieval times. But one of the most unique churches in the country is a more contemporary structure that goes by the name of Wotruba Church. This church has a Cubist style and was created in the 1970s, resembling a kind of futuristic Stonehenge. Although you wouldn't even expect the building to be a church, we do find it very beautiful.

(Ottillingerpl. 1, 1230 Vienna; www.georgenberg.at)

90. Take Waltz Lessons at Tanzschule Elmayer

The Viennese Waltz is the original form of the waltz, and one of the most stunningly beautiful ballroom dances to see. While you're in Vienna you should have no problems seeking out a waltz performance, but how much cooler would it be if you could actually learn how to perform this stunning dance while you're in Vienna? Fortunately, you can. Tanzschule Elmayer is a school that offers group and private lessons so that you can done your dance skills and waltz like a pro.

(Bräunerstraße 13, 1010 Vienna; https://elmayer.at/en)

91. Explore the Roman Playground of Carnuntum

If you are not the kind of person who gets their kicks from visiting ancient ruins, we think that the ruins complex of Carnuntum might be the place to change your mind. Why? This Roman Legionary Fortress was a large city of 50,000 inhabitants, and now much of the city has been recreated faithfully where the city stood all those many years ago with incredible depictions of kitchens, baths, early heating systems, and more. Totally fascinating.

(Hauptstraße 1A, 2404 Petronell-Carnuntum; www.carnuntum.at/en)

92. Get up Close to Mozart's Skull

The pride and joy of Salzburg is, of course, the world famous classical composer, Wolfgang Mozart. There are plenty of opportunities to enjoy Mozart recitals in this city, but if you are a super-fan, be sure to find your way to the University Mozarteum, a university that specialises in music and the performing arts. Mozart's skull is on display at the university museum, or at least it is said to be his skull but as yet there is no conclusive proof that it belongs to the great composer.

(Mirabellplatz 1, 5020 Salzburg)

93. Enjoy Authentic Sachertorte at Café Sacher

If you can't get indulgent and decadent on your holiday in Austria, then when can you? And that's why we stuff Sachertorte into our gobs pretty much around the clock when we are in Austria. If you're unfamiliar with this glorious Austrian dessert, it's a very dense chocolate cake with a thin layer of apricot jam on top, and then the whole thing is coated in dark chocolate ganache. It was invented in 1832 for Prince Sacher, and Café Sacher in Salzburg is the place to chow down on the best slice of your life.

(Hotel Sacher, Schwarzstraße 5-7, 5020 Salzburg; www.sacher.com/hotel-salzburg/kulinarik-2/cafe-sacher-salzburg)

94. Feel Festive at Salzburg's Christmas Market

Austria is a country that has four very defined seasons. Of course, the most popular time to visit is the summer when there are long, sunny days. But we think that December has its own charm, because there are few countries that are more festive than Austria. You'll be able to find Christmas markets up and down the country, but we think our favourite might just be the annual Salzburg Christmas market. The origins of the Chriskindlmarkt date all the way back to the late 15th century, and it's still incredibly popular with wonderful food and drink, outdoor carol concerts, festive decorations, gift shopping, and loads more besides.

(Residenzpl., 5020 Salzburg; www.christkindlmarkt.co.at)

95. Watch a Puppet Show at Salzburg's Marionette Theatre

You probably didn't venture all the way to Austria to check out different puppet shows, but if you do have an hour or two spare in Salzburg, we think that the local Marionette Theatre is actually really entertaining, and it's the real deal because it just so happens to be one of the oldest continuing Marionette theatres in the world, now open for over a century. They put on a variety of operas, ballets, other productions, and cater to kids and adults.

(Schwarzstraße 24, 5020 Salzburg; www.marionetten.at)

96. Have a Thrilling Toboggan Ride at the Fisser Flitzer

Feel like injecting some serious adrenaline levels into your Austria trip? Then you absolutely need to find your way to Fisser Flitzer, the country's summer dry toboggan run. This fun toboggan run starts at a crazy altitude of over 1800 metres, extends for over 2 kilometres, and you'll reach speeds of up to 45 kilometres/hour as you race down the hill.

(Möseralm, 6533 Fiss; www.serfaus-fiss-ladis.at/en/summer/highlights/flitzer-flieger-skyswing)

97. Get Close to Wildlife at Innsbruck Alpine Zoo

When you visit a zoo, you probably expect to find all kinds of exotic animals like tigers and giraffes, but the Innsbruck Alpine Zoo is completely dedicated to Alpine animals that you can find in Austria and Central Europe. This zoo is well known for its conservation efforts and commitment to biodiversity, and once inside you'll find beautiful brown bears, stunning lynx cats, soaring golden eagles, and many other beautiful creatures besides.

(Weiherburggasse 37a, 6020 Innsbruck; www.alpenzoo.at)

98. Sip on a Strong Glass of Sturm

When we visit a new country, we love nothing more than to explore the local tipples and really drink like a local. Everybody knows that Austrians enjoy a pint of beer or two, but what about Sturm? This is a local drink that you might not have heard about. This is partly because you can only drink it from the end of September to mid-October. It is basically a young wine, or fermented grape juice, and it's enjoyed in vineyards across the country.

99. Take a Scenic Train Ride From Vienna to Graz

In a beautiful country like Austria, sometimes getting from A to B is just as enjoyable as doing things in a particular destination. There are many scenic train rides that you can enjoy across the country, and we think that the journey from Vienna to Graz (or the other way, of course) is very beautiful indeed. On the three house journey, you'll get to see glistening mountaintops, dense forests, green valleys, and plenty of the local wildlife.

100. Enjoy Smooth Jazz Sounds at Jazz Fest Wien

If you can't get enough of the smooth sounds of jazz, it's a great idea to visit Austria at the end of June when the Jazz Fest Wien takes place each year. This jazz festival has been going strong since 1991, and is now considered to be one of the best jazz festivals anywhere in the world. All kinds of jazz are represented, from swing to experimental jazz and everything in between, and big names that have taken to the festival stage include Herbie Hancock, Dionne Warwick, and George Benson.

(www.jazzfest.wien/en)

101. Adventure Through the Tirol Mountain Bike Safari

Want to have a true adventure and immerse yourself in the stunning landscapes of the Alps? Then you need to know about the Tirol Mountain Bike Safari. This long distance route crosses 670 kilometres of very hilly terrain so it is certainly not for the faint hearted. There are, however, sixteen stages to the safari, so if you just wanted to pick out a couple of these you could do that. However you enjoy the bike safari, it will be a journey to remember.

(www.tyrol.com/things-to-do/sports/mountainbiking/bikesafari)

Before You Go...

Thanks for reading **101 Amazing Things to Do in Austria.** We hope that it makes your trip a memorable one!

Have a great trip, and don't eat too much schnitzel!

Team 101 Amazing Things

Printed in Great Britain
by Amazon